Mount Pleasant

Sullivan's Island

Fort Moultrie

Fort Sumter

Cumming's Point Battery

THE ESCAPE OF ROBERT SMALLS

A Daring Voyage Out of Slavery

by Jehan Jones-Radgowski

illustrated by Poppy Kang

CAPSTONE EDITIONS

a capstone imprint

On the evening of May 12, 1862, Charleston Harbor echoed with the sounds of dusk at the docks. Men murmured to one another as they retired from a long day's work. Crickets chirped. Water lapped against ships.

But underneath the peaceful concert was the *thump, thump, thump* of Robert Smalls's racing heart.

Robert Smalls was born into slavery. Enslaved people were considered the legal property of another person. Almost four million black people were enslaved at the time of the Civil War. They had no rights. They lived and worked in brutal conditions. They received no pay.

The atmosphere was tense on that dark, foggy evening.

The Confederate army was fighting against the Union army. Southern Confederates wanted to secede from the United States. Slavery was legal in the South, and those states wanted to keep it. Union troops from the North fought to keep the U.S. together. The Union wanted to outlaw slavery.

The Union navy was blockading Charleston, South Carolina. Confederate ships, forts, and soldiers were on guard. They were ready to protect the city from enemy attacks.

Charles Relyea was the captain of the Confederate steamship *Planter*. He decided to take a break for the night to visit with family. As on many other nights, Relyea left Robert Smalls in charge.

Captains were supposed to stay on their ships. They were expected to be ready to sail at a moment's notice. If Relyea were caught, he could face a court-martial. He might lose command of his ship.

Smalls saluted Relyea and the other white officers as they

Smalls knew Charleston Harbor as well as anyone.

When he was twelve years old, Smalls was sent by his owner to look for a job in Charleston. He worked at the waterfront, performing many different jobs on the boats. While he worked, Smalls carefully watched the crews and learned their responsibilities. He earned sixteen dollars a month, but most of it went to his owner. Smalls negotiated with his owner to keep a small amount for himself.

In 1861, Smalls was hired as a crewmember on the *Planter*. He quickly mastered skills such as line handling, knot tying, and getting under way. He learned how to secure ships at the docks with ropes and chains. These skills would help Smalls as he moved up the ranks.

Smalls worked hard to memorize the ship routes. He learned where hazards existed in the harbor, such as sandbars under the surface of the water. Because Smalls was enslaved, he was not recognized as the ship's pilot. But he performed these duties regularly.

His highest position was wheelman. As the wheelman, Smalls steered the ship.

On a typical night, Smalls would clean and organize the ship for the next day. But tonight was not a typical night.

Smalls was preparing to carry out a dangerous plan.

Smalls's crewmates said that he had gotten the idea to steal the Confederate steamship months before. Smalls had stood near the wheel of the steamship one day. One of his crewmates put a big straw hat on Smalls's head. Someone joked that he looked like Captain Relyea. Both men had short, stocky builds. They folded their arms in a similar manner.

Smalls began to carefully observe Relyea at the helm. He took note of the captain's movements. He memorized the signals required to pass checkpoints. He studied how Relyea moved his hands on the wheel. He copied the way he tilted his hat. He practiced until he was able to mimic the captain perfectly.

On May 12, 1862, Captain Relyea had left that very hat and one of his uniforms on the ship. Around three in the morning on the thirteenth, Smalls donned the captain's uniform. He pulled the wide-brimmed straw hat low on his forehead. He hunched over the wheel like the captain did. He was ready to put his training to use.

The spring night sky was inky black. Fog filled the air. Seeing where the sky ended and the murky waters began was almost impossible. The conditions were perfect for Smalls's escape.

Smalls and the rest of the crew were taking a big risk.
They would steal a Confederate ship and sail it toward
the Union blockade. If all went as planned, they would
eventually enter Union territory.

No person had done this before. They would pass armed
forts, where soldiers were on alert. They would risk their
lives, all for the chance to be free.

Smalls enlisted the help of the other enslaved crewmen.
He planned to bring their families to freedom. But there
was great risk involved.

Steamboats make lots of noise and smoke as they move
through water. Sneaking unnoticed past the forts would
be impossible. Because they couldn't sneak, they'd have to
boldly sail right under the Confederates' noses.

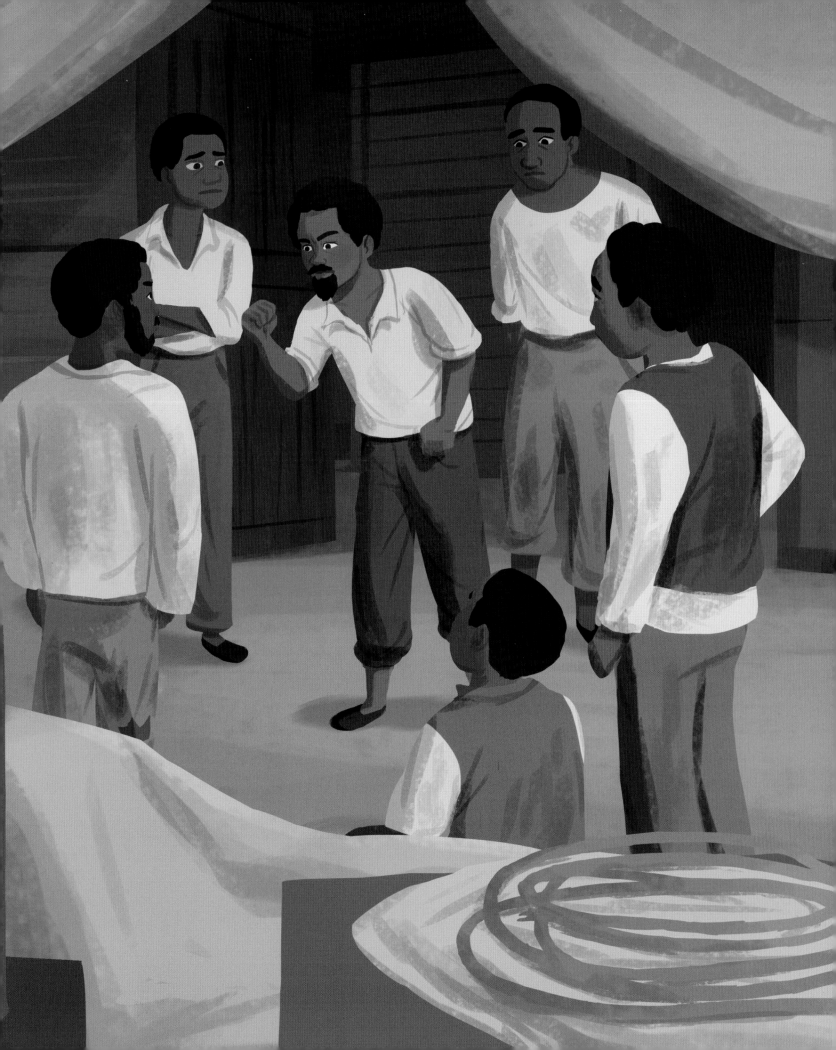

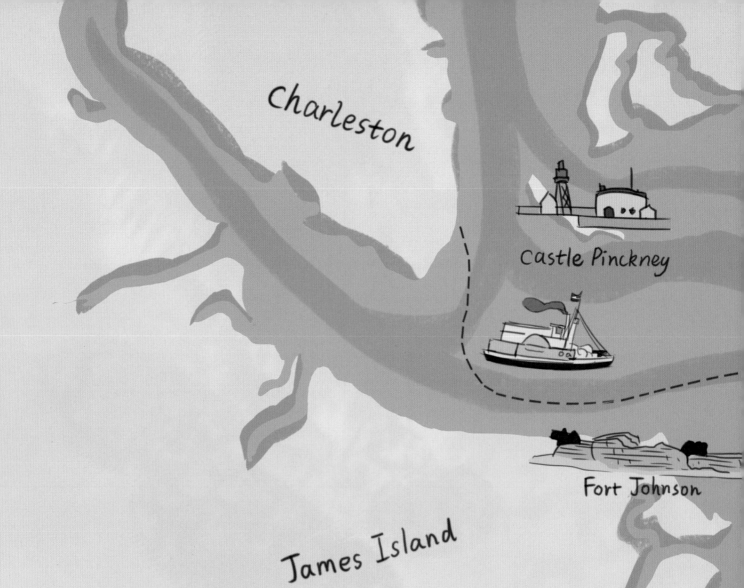

Charleston

Castle Pinckney

Fort Johnson

James Island

Morris Island

The *Planter* would follow a ten-mile route. The beginning of the voyage would take place within view of General Ripley's headquarters. General Ripley was the commander for Charleston. He was in charge of military vessels in the harbor.

Then they would need to pass several Confederate forts. Soldiers with guns would be standing guard. They would be ready to shoot. Only when the *Planter* passed those forts would they have the chance to enter Union-controlled waters.

Mount Pleasant

Sullivan's Island

Fort Moultrie

Fort Sumter

Cumming's Point Battery

Smalls knew they would also need to act quickly once the *Planter* approached the Union fleet. Union forces might mistake them for enemy soldiers and fire on them.

There was danger on all sides.

If caught by the Confederacy, Smalls and the other runaways would be punished harshly.

The Confederates relied on the *Planter*. It was used to transport personnel and supplies to the forts around the harbor. In fact, the *Planter* had just been loaded with artillery the previous day. Two hundred pounds of ammunition were on board the ship, plus guns and cannons. The weapons were supposed to be delivered to forts later that day.

The Confederate military would rather sink the *Planter* than see all those weapons land in enemy hands.

Smalls would rather use the weaponry to fight to the death than allow himself to be captured.

The families of the crewmen waited in secret at the North Atlantic Wharf. Smalls's wife and children were among them. They hid inside another boat at the wharf until the *Planter* arrived.

Years before, Smalls had tried to buy his family's freedom. At the time, he didn't have the money. But now he was enacting a new plan to gain their freedom.

If they succeeded, the reward would be priceless.

As the crew prepared to set sail, two of the crewmen became very frightened. Runaway slaves were often whipped. They could be sold into harsher conditions or even killed. The two men decided to leave the ship.

The remaining seven crewmen worried. Would their departing crewmates give away the escape plans?

But Smalls carried on. He ordered the crew to prepare for departure.

They piled wood into a stove to boil water and produce steam. The steam created energy to move the boat. On deck, the crew hoisted the Confederate flag and the South Carolina flag to maintain their disguise.

The *Planter* set off toward the North Atlantic
Wharf, moving in a different direction from its
typical route. Luckily no one seemed to notice.

The steamship paused at the wharf. The
crewmembers' families sneaked off the boat they
were hiding in and climbed aboard the *Planter*.
A total of sixteen runaway slaves were now aboard.

PLANTER

The steamer cranked, hissed, and whistled as it got
underway. Every time it made a noise, the passengers
held their breath. They prayed no one noticed anything
suspicious.

Smalls steered the boat toward Fort Johnson. It was the
first of two heavily armed forts they would pass. The crew
steeled themselves for whatever was to come.

Fort Johnson was about two miles away, on James Island. To the *Planter* crew, that distance felt like two thousand miles. The fort had cannonball-firing mortars and soldiers on guard. The soldiers were armed with guns.

As the *Planter* sailed close to Fort Johnson, the crewmen braced themselves for gunfire. They crouched and covered their heads, waiting for cannonballs to pound the ship. But the guards at Fort Johnson were tired. They noticed nothing out of the ordinary. The *Planter* sailed past the fort safely.

The crew quietly celebrated. Fort Johnson was their first big test.

But as the *Planter* sailed on, Smalls's crew noticed a Confederate guard boat ahead. The guard boat monitored activity in the area. The crew of the guard boat had no idea the *Planter* carried runaway slaves.

Smalls remained calm. He stood in the small cabin atop the *Planter* and saluted the other captain. Then he tugged at the rope to sound the whistle as they passed. Smalls even shouted a greeting to the pilot.

The *Planter* crew had succeeded again.

The biggest challenge still lay before them.

Soldiers at Fort Sumter looked out for suspicious activity. They were instructed to destroy any enemy vessels.

Fort Sumter was where the first shots of the Civil War had been fired thirteen months before.

The fort was surrounded by walls that reached fifty feet above the water. Loaded cannons were all around.

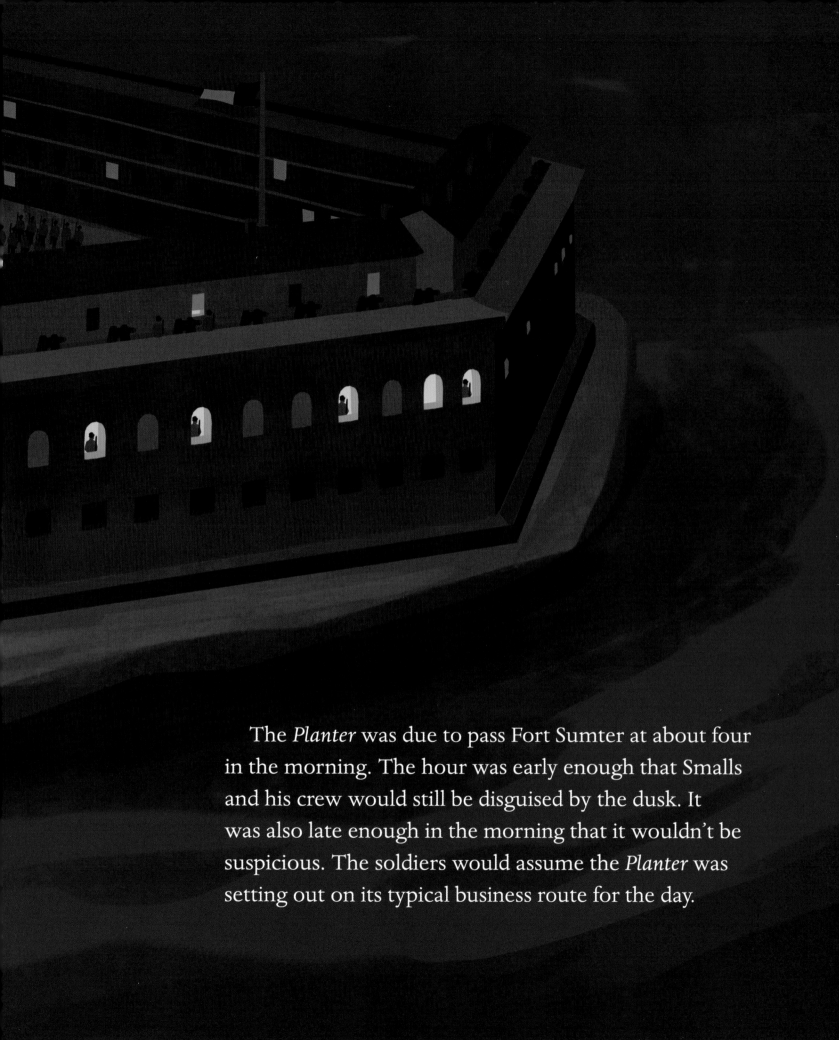

The *Planter* was due to pass Fort Sumter at about four in the morning. The hour was early enough that Smalls and his crew would still be disguised by the dusk. It was also late enough in the morning that it wouldn't be suspicious. The soldiers would assume the *Planter* was setting out on its typical business route for the day.

Up ahead logs floated in the water, blocking the Planter's path. Smalls had to steer the ship very close to the walls of Fort Sumter to avoid them. The people on board the *Planter* held their breath, terrified. One person said he felt as if he was a rabbit in front of a dog. Some of the crew fell to the deck. They covered their heads, expecting cannon fire. Others stood still and grabbed hold of their pants to keep their hands from shaking.

But not Robert Smalls.

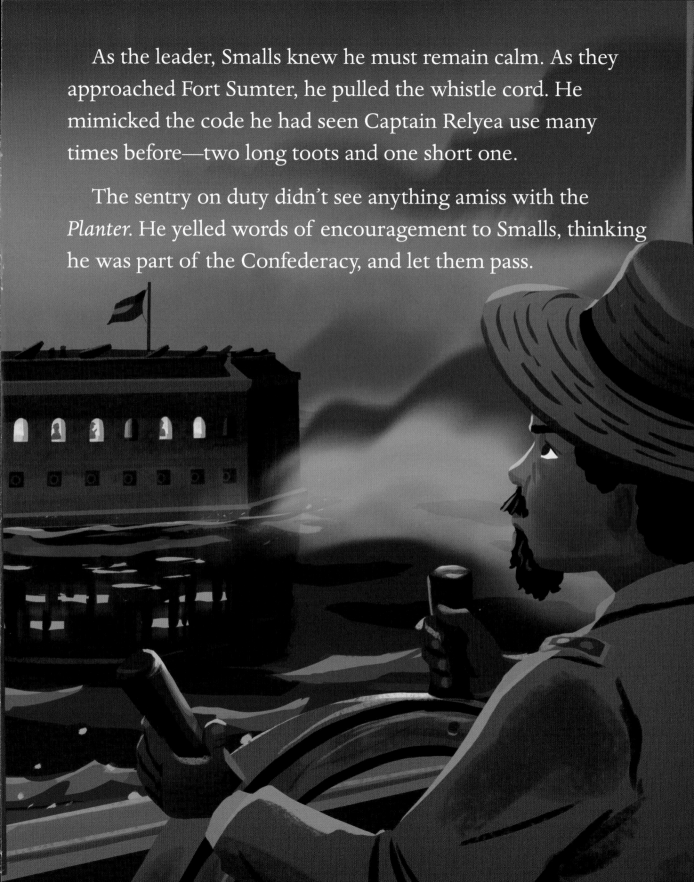

As the leader, Smalls knew he must remain calm. As they approached Fort Sumter, he pulled the whistle cord. He mimicked the code he had seen Captain Relyea use many times before—two long toots and one short one.

The sentry on duty didn't see anything amiss with the *Planter*. He yelled words of encouragement to Smalls, thinking he was part of the Confederacy, and let them pass.

But minutes later, the soldiers noticed something unusual. The *Planter* was going the wrong way. It was supposed to take supplies to Morris Island. Instead the ship was sailing toward the Union fleet. Now the soldiers knew something was wrong. They tried to fire on Smalls and his crew, but the steamer was too far away

They signaled to Morris Island to fire, but those cannons were also out of firing range. The Confederate soldiers could do nothing but watch as the *Planter* sailed toward the Union ships.

The runaways finally let their shoulders drop. Some wept with relief. Others danced, prayed, or sang. But they quickly ended their celebration. Their dangerous journey was not yet over.

Smalls knew they could easily be mistaken for Confederate troops. He ordered the Confederate and South Carolina flags lowered as they approached the Union ships. In their place, Smalls instructed his crew to raise a white bedsheet. This would signal their peaceful surrender.

The *Onward*, a Union warship, sat ahead. The *Planter* was headed directly for it. Aboard the Union ship, Captain John Frederick Nickels called out to his crew, "All hands to quarters!"

He planned to destroy the enemy ship before it destroyed his own.

The fog had helped Smalls earlier, but it was not helping now. The morning haze made it difficult for the Union soldiers to see the white flag. They couldn't tell that the men on board the *Planter* were not enemy soldiers.

The *Onward* crew could only see that there was a warship headed toward them. It was coming from enemy territory.

Roughly one hundred Union sailors on the *Onward* were now awake. They raced to their battle stations.

The Union soldiers aimed their cannons toward the *Planter*. They waited for Nickels to give the order.

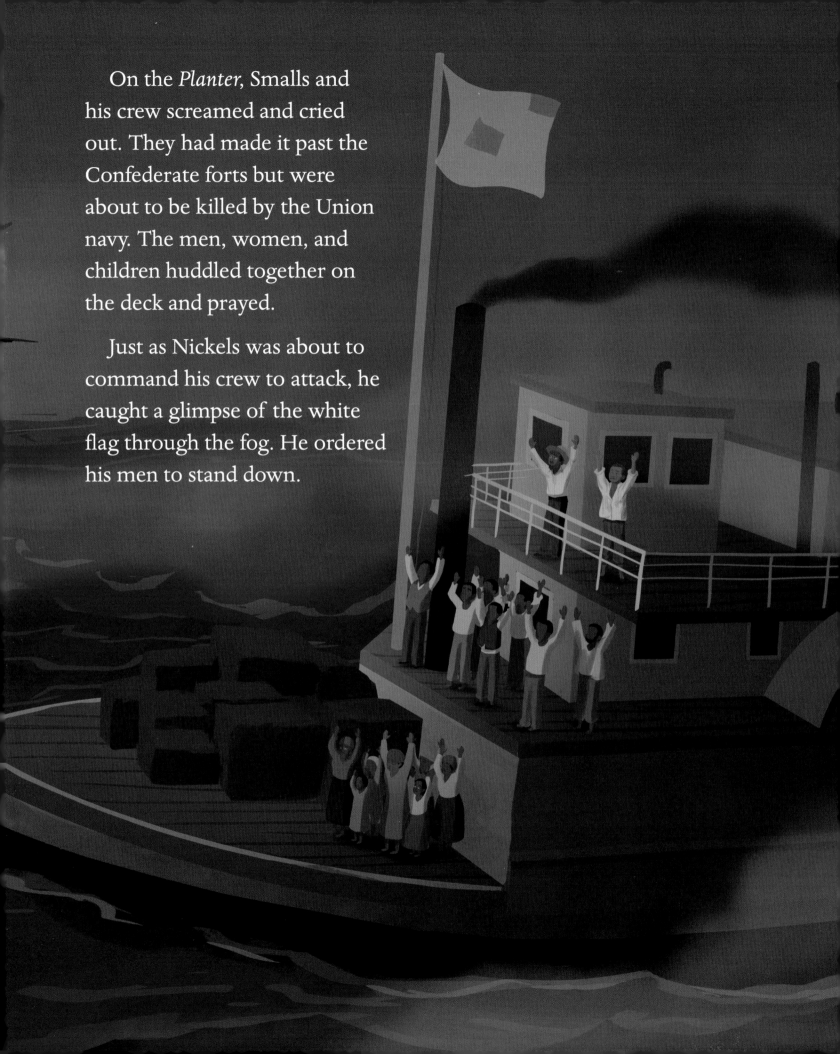

On the *Planter*, Smalls and his crew screamed and cried out. They had made it past the Confederate forts but were about to be killed by the Union navy. The men, women, and children huddled together on the deck and prayed.

Just as Nickels was about to command his crew to attack, he caught a glimpse of the white flag through the fog. He ordered his men to stand down.

The wheelman steered the *Planter* alongside the *Onward*. Smalls shouted, "Good morning, sir! I've brought you some of the old United States' guns, sir!"

For a few moments, the *Planter* crew was frozen. Then it hit them—they were out of danger.

Joy broke out among the crew and the passengers. "Hallelujah!" one of the women shouted. A group of men jumped and danced. A child who'd fallen asleep during the adventure woke to happy shouts and songs of merriment.

Smalls looked over at the exuberant crew and smiled. His heart beat loudly and proudly. He had done it.

Freedom, at last.

AFTERWORD

Robert Smalls was born April 5, 1839, in Beaufort, South Carolina. Like his mother, he was enslaved. Slavery was a system that allowed people to buy and own other human beings. Enslaved people had no rights. They were not allowed to decide what they would wear or eat, or what job they would do.

The system of slavery in America began in 1619, when Dutch settlers brought captured African men and women to Jamestown, Virginia. Throughout the seventeenth and eighteenth centuries, white settlers bought enslaved people to help farm their land, first for tobacco and later for cotton production.

Many people thought slavery was wrong. An abolitionist was a person whose goal was to outlaw slavery. Many abolitionists advocated for immediate emancipation, or freeing, of all slaves. By 1804, slavery was outlawed in all northern states. In 1807, a law passed that said the slave trade would end in 1808. But slavery continued on U.S. soil for many more decades.

Many slaves dreamed of traveling north to free states. But to escape successfully was uncommon. The Fugitive Slave Acts of 1793 and 1850 said that runaway enslaved people could be captured and returned to their masters. Enslaved people who returned often received harsh and painful punishments. As a result of the Fugitive Slave Act, some free black people in the North, including children, were kidnapped, taken to the South, and enslaved.

The Southern states and the Northern states had different opinions on many topics, including the rights of states and the role of the federal government. Eventually, many Southern states decided to secede from the United States. The Southern states decided to form their own country. They called it the Confederacy, or the Confederate States of America. The Confederacy included eleven states— South Carolina, Mississippi, Florida, Alabama, Georgia, Louisiana, Texas, Virginia, Arkansas, North Carolina, and Tennessee. In 1861, the Confederate States declared war against the United States, or the Union.

The Northern and Southern states fought from 1861 to 1865 in the American Civil War, with battles and raids from Vermont to New Mexico. The war began on April 12, 1861, when Confederate soldiers attacked Union soldiers at Fort Sumter, South Carolina—the very fort Robert Smalls would sneak by a year later, disguised as Captain Relyea.

Almost 200,000 African Americans fought in the Civil War. Robert Smalls was among them. After escaping to the North, Smalls joined the Union navy. He eventually became the first black captain of a U.S. military ship. Smalls fought in seventeen battles against the Confederacy and recruited African Americans to become soldiers for the Union.

In 1863, President Abraham Lincoln issued the Emancipation Proclamation. This document declared enslaved people in rebel states to be free.

The Civil War was brutal, and both sides lost many lives. At least 752,000 people died. Ten thousand battles were fought. On April 9, 1865, Confederate General Robert E. Lee surrendered, and other Confederate generals soon followed.

However, the ending of the war did not end slavery. It wasn't until December 1865, when the Thirteenth Amendment to the U.S. Constitution was ratified, that slavery was outlawed on a national scale.

Robert Smalls returned to South Carolina and bought his former slaveholder's home. The U.S. Navy gave Smalls $1,500 for capturing the Confederate ship and delivering it to the Union.

Smalls became a politician and served in the U.S. House of Representatives. He died in 1915, a retired U.S. congressman and U.S. Navy captain. But gaining freedom for himself and his family—against all odds—was perhaps his greatest accomplishment.

GLOSSARY

ammunition (am-yuh-NISH-uhn)—things that can be fired from weapons, such as bullets

artillery (ahr-TIL-ur-ee)—large guns that are mounted on wheels or tracks

blockade (blah-KADE)—the closing off of an area to keep people or supplies from going in or out

checkpoint (CHEK-poynt)—a barrier where travelers are subject to security checks

court-martial (KORT-MAHR-shuhl)—a court in which members of the military are put on trial

enlisted (en-LIST-id)—got someone's help

hazard (HA-zurd)—something that is dangerous or likely to cause problems

helm (helm)—the wheel or handle used to steer a boat

mimic (MI-mik)—to imitate someone else

mortar (MOR-tur)—a heavy gun that fires cannonballs, shells, or rockets

personnel (purr-suh-NEL)—people who work for the military or other organization

ratified (RAT-ih-fide)—agreed to or approved officially

secede (si-SEED)—to formally withdraw from a group or organization, often to form another organization

READ MORE

Kimmel, Allison Crotzer. *A Primary Source History of Slavery in the United States.* Primary Source History. North Mankato, MN: Capstone Press, 2015.

Lakin, Patricia. *Heroes Who Risked Everything for Freedom: The Civil War.* Secrets of American History. New York: Simon Spotlight, 2017.

Meriwether, Louise. *The Freedom Ship of Robert Smalls.* Young Palmetto Books. Columbia: University of South Carolina Press, 2018.

ABOUT THE AUTHOR

Jehan Jones-Radgowski is a U.S. foreign service officer. She has lived all over the world, including South Africa, Spain, Venezuela, Ghana, and the Dominican Republic. She is from Petersburg, Virginia, where the largest number of African American troops were stationed during the Civil War. Jehan is an active member of the Society of Children's Book Writers and Illustrators. She currently lives in Germany with her family.

ABOUT THE ILLUSTRATOR

Poppy Kang is an illustrator and background artist with a passion to create artwork that has meaningful messages and cinematic lighting. She was born in China and developed her illustration talent at Art Center College of Design in Pasadena, California. Poppy is currently based in Los Angeles, California.

Charleston

Castle Pinckney

Fort Johnson

James Island

Morris
Island

The Escape of Robert Smalls is published by
Capstone Editions, a Capstone imprint
1710 Roe Crest Drive
North Mankato, Minnesota 56003
www.mycapstone.com

Library of Congress Cataloging-in-Publication Data
Names: Jones-Radgowski, Jehan, author. | Kang, Poppy, illustrator.
Title: The escape of Robert Smalls : a perilous voyage out of
    slavery / by Jehan Jones-Radgowski ; illustrated by Poppy Kang.
Description: North Mankato, Minnesota : Capstone Editions,
    [2019] | Includes bibliographical references.
Identifiers: LCCN 2018049848| ISBN 9781543512816
    (hardcover) | ISBN 9781543512892 (ebook pdf)
Subjects: LCSH: Smalls, Robert, 1839-1915. | Slaves—South
    Carolina—Biography—Juvenile literature. | Escapes—South
    Carolina—Juvenile literature—Juvenile literature. | African
    Americans—South Carolina—Biography—Juvenile literature. |
    African American sailors—Biography—Juvenile literature. |
    United States—History—Civil War, 1861-1865—Biography—
    Juvenile literature. | United States—History—Civil War,
    1861-1865—Participation, African American—Juvenile
    literature.
Classification: LCC E185.97.S6 J66 2019 | DDC 973.8092 [B] —dc23
LC record available at https://lccn.loc.gov/2018049848

Image Credits: Library of Congress/Prints & Photographs Division
(page 37); Stephanie Reese of Reese Studios (author photo)
Artistic elements: Shutterstock: Andrew Angelov, ANURAK
PONGPATIMET, Martina I. Meyer, rubikphoto

Thanks to our adviser for his expertise, research, and advice:
Dr. W. Marvin Dulaney
Associate Professor of History Emeritus
University of Texas, Arlington

Editor: Eliza Leahy
Designer: Ted Williams

Printed and bound in China
001669

Selected Bibliography

Billingsley, Andrew. *Yearning to Breathe Free: Robert
Smalls and His Families.* Columbia: University of South
Carolina Press, 2007.

"Civil War Facts." American Battlefield Trust. Accessed
Dec. 27, 2018, https://www.battlefields.org/learn/
articles/civil-war-facts.

Gates Jr., Henry Louis. "Which Slave Sailed Himself to
Freedom?" Accessed June 11, 2017, http://www.pbs.
org/wnet/african-americans-many-rivers-to-cross/
history/which-slave-sailed-himself-to-freedom/.

Lineberry, Cate. *Be Free or Die: The Amazing Story of
Robert Smalls' Escape from Slavery to Union Hero.* New
York: St. Martin's Press, 2017.

McPherson, James M. *The Negro's Civil War: How
American Blacks Felt and Acted During the War for the
Union.* Vintage Civil War Library. New York: Vintage
Books, 2003.

Miller, Edward A. Jr., *Gullah Statesman: Robert Smalls
from Slavery to Congress, 1839–1915.* Columbia:
University of South Carolina Press, 1995.

"Smalls, Robert. 1839 to 1915." The Frederick Douglass
Papers at the Library of Congress, Feb. 22, 1915.
Manuscript/Mixed Material. Accessed June 03, 2017,
https://www.loc.gov/item/mfd.19024/.

"The Steamer Planter and Her Captor." *Harper's Weekly,*
June 14, 1862. Page 372. Photograph. Accessed Dec. 27,
2018, https://www.loc.gov/resource/cph.3c17998/

Source Notes

p. 30, "All hands to quarters!" James M. Guthrie. *Camp-
Fires of the Afro-American.* Philadelphia: Afro-American
pub. co., 1899, p. 312.

p. 34, "Good morning, sir!..." Guthrie. *Camp-Fires of the
Afro-American,* p. 313.